RUGBY REMEMBERED
MORE IMAGES OF RUGBY

RUGBY REMEMBERED
MORE IMAGES OF RUGBY

breedon **books**
PUBLISHING

First published in Great Britain in 2005 by

The Breedon Books Publishing Company Limited

Breedon House, 3 The Parker Centre, Derby, DE21 4SZ.

ISBN 1 85983 490 6

Printed and bound by Cromwell Press, Trowbridge, Wiltshire

Contents

Introduction   7

The Rugby Advertiser   9

Then and now   10

Places   25

People and Groups   47

Memorable Events   61

More Rugby Events   71

Sporting   91

School Photographs   108

Industry and Working in Rugby   123

Miscellaneous Photographs   142

Acknowledgements

We would like to thank everyone who has contributed towards this work, particularly the following sources for their help in providing pictures and information: Rugby School archives department, Rugby Museum, members of the public who have loaned photographs and the many avid followers of the Advertiser's Looking Back feature.

Introduction

By Rugby Advertiser Editor Peter Aengenheister

Welcome to Rugby Remembered, our follow-up to Images of Rugby, which we published in 1996 in celebration of the Rugby Advertiser''s 150th anniversary.

The opportunity to produce this second volume came mainly as a result of a huge amount of interest in the last one, and because over the past nine years we have had many enquiries about when we might bring out another. So here it is and I hope you like it.

Finding 'new' pictures of old Rugby has been a difficult trawl, and we are always looking for different views. So if you are inspired by this volume and you would like to contribute to a future one we would be delighted to scan your contribution, which we will save in our files.

Probably the most significant event to affect Rugby since 'Images' has been that the England rugby team won the World Cup, the Webb Ellis Trophy, and, along with some of the team, England Manager Sir Clive Woodward came to the town with the cup.

Also momentous in that time has been the closure of Rugby's BT masts site and the felling of all but eight of the giant masts that have dominated the local skyline for years. And thirdly the gutting of Avon Valley School when it was ravaged by fire.

But this book, like the first, is mainly a look at Rugby's earlier days, or at least as early as photographs will allow. By definition this means that the oldest pictures are around the turn of the century.

Preceeding that, though, I should just remind our readers of the key dates in the town's history.

1255 – the real start of Rugby's development.

1567 – Local greengrocer Lawrence Sheriff founded Rugby School.

1605 – Guy Fawkes, who had a house in Dunchurch, and his pals gathered in an upper room at Ashby St Ledgers House to hatch the Gun Powder Plot to destroy The Houses of Parliament and the majority of its members.

1645 – The Battle of Naseby.

1823 – The Close, Rugby School student William Webb Ellis founded the game of rugby when he 'picked up the ball and ran'.

Early 60s – The arrival of the M1 motorway.

Early 90s – The completion of the A14 east coast link.

Despite the impact of the Beeching cuts to railways in the 60s, Rugby's station survived and the railway continues to be a vital connection for business and commuters.

The Rugby Advertiser
Serving the community since 1846

Coming up to its 160th anniversary, the Rugby Advertiser, the town's only paid-for weekly newspaper, remains a cornerstone of the community, faithfully reporting news, views and sport throughout the years.

The paper started life in March 1846, founded by William Ironside Tait. Over the years it has been run by several publishing companies but is currently published by Heart of England Newspapers.

New technology has streamlined the operation to a large extent and editorially pages are completed ready for the press by the staff in the Rugby office. Some typesetting for adverts still has to be done by our pre-press unit in Northampton.

Current Editor of the Rugby Advertiser is Peter Aengenheister and the Advertisement Manager is Ginny Hunter.

Being a news and information business ,the Rugby Advertiser has embraced the innovation of the worldwide web. The Rugby Advertiser's online pages, which you can find by logging on to www.rugbytoday.co.uk, give a vast amount of news, information, special features and links and it is updated regularly. The paper is printed in Peterborough and is on sale first thing every Thursday.

The current staff are:

EDITOR:	Peter Aengenheidter	ADVERTISEMENT MANAGER:	Ginny Hunter
EDITORIAL:		**REPRESENTATIVES:**	
Assistant Editor	Gordon Birch	Sales Manager	Lisa Bedford
Sports Editor	Zoe Ashton		
News Editor	Lucie Green	Motors (Senior)	Julie Haynes
Reporter	Phil Hibble	Key Accounts Manager/Property	Leasa Marriott
Reporter	Stuart Turner	Expert Services and Motors	Lisa Hurst
Chief Photographer	Mike Baker	Retail	Sian Leyshon
Photographer	Ian Spencer	Retail	Laura Fordham
Editorial Assistant	Kate Harris	Key Events/Special Projects Manager	Jo Billings
CLASSIFIED:		**RECEPTION:**	
Property/classified	Michelle Dawson	Michelle Allen (Senior Receptionist)	
Recruitment	Liz Friel	Nikki Allett	
Expert Services	Tiffany Baines	Kerry Marriott	
Expert Services	Jayde Beck		
Entertainments	Hollie Langstone	**NEWSPAPER SALES AND PROMOTIONS**	
		Newspaper Sales Manager	Terri Short
ADMINISTRATORS:	Michelle Crozier-Foxon	Newspaper Sales Administrator	Sue Booth

Then and Now

Above and below: The entrance to the churchyard of St Peter's Church, just beyond The Green, Dunchurch.

In the old picture above the trees on Hillmorton Green are mere saplings, today though they have reached maturity. Little else seems to have changed over the years.

The spring of 1958, this picture was taken from West Street and shows what is now Corporation Street, below, under construction. A Galliford's sign warns the traffic it is a no through road and of the 'DANGER AHEAD'. Today the modern street scene makes the site unrecognisable.

The Green at Dunchurch with its old stocks and bus shelter, with the old coaching inn, The Dun Cow, behind on the left. Today the stocks have been moved to another part of The Green and a new bus shelter has been built.

Here we have a view along Clifton Road. The picture is taken from opposite The Squirrel pub in the late 50s. The top picture shows shops on the left, including Walkers Fruit Stores (see below), but they have now made way for the Gas Street car park (see below).

Caldecott Park – not a lot of changes here. The band stand remains a central feature, the main changes being the seating and the planting itself.

The trees on Clifton Road that still stand outside Lawrence Sheriff School once formed part of an impressive boulevard of trees.

In this shot of Church Street taken from the entrance of Albert Street, it appears that there has been very little change over the years, but in the older picture of the street there is a Belisha Beacon. In the recent one the scene is strewn with street 'furniture'.

The Crown and The Rugby Tavern have been successful plying their trade since this old shot was taken in around 1900. Some quite extensive development was made to The Crown at some time. Still with three storeys, it suddenly grew much taller – compare it to the building to the left, which is now the Abbey National building.

The corner of Little Church Street and Hillmorton Road has changed considerably. The older picture – we are not sure when it was taken but believe it was before the turn of the century – has a group of pupils from The School, and the building on the site was then one of the boarding houses.

Inside the grounds of Rugby School, a view of the ivy-covered edifice of the Head Master's residence doesn't change much – except where the ivy grows and the introduction of cars.

The pupils at Rugby School enjoy games of cricket. No one is suggesting that this picture was taken before William Webb Ellis picked up the ball and ran, but, apart from it possibly being a different time of year, the sport has changed to that for which the school is better known.

Taken in 1965, this picture of Rugby Station shows what it was like in its heyday, but it was actually when the Beeching Report declared that the demand for using the railways had waned and that it was no longer the future for transport. Nevertheless, despite continued increases in ticket prices and a decline in services, Rugby Station is well used.

The junction of Corporation Street and Lawford Road, which was Warwick Street, Addison Row and Lawford Road.

A view down Church Street towards the Clock Tower.

Places

A lack of traffic makes Rugby's Church Street look totally different at the end of the 19th century.

A broader view of Rugby's Church Street when bicycles were the most popular form of transport.

A shot of High Street looking toward Rugby School. Note the absence of vehicles.

Victorian Rugby – Horses, carts and carriages visit the shops in High Street, pictured in a view looking toward the Market Square.

Looking into the Market Square towards the Clock Tower from the junction of High Street and Sheep Street, Foster brothers on the left became Millets, Barclays on the right is now Monsoon and further on that side is now W.H. Smith.

The Forester's Arms, which stood on the corner of West Street and West Leys, now Corporation Street. The landlord at the time this picture was taken was Mr George Gill.

Prior to the 1950s, this establishment was known as Dunsmore Secondary School, then it became Ashlawn School, Ashlawn Road, Rugby.

A picture we believe was taken in 1905 from the top of Holy Trinity Church (which was knocked down after a fire in 1980). It shows the wide straight road that is Railway Terrace, and in the left forefront is the entrance to Gas Street.

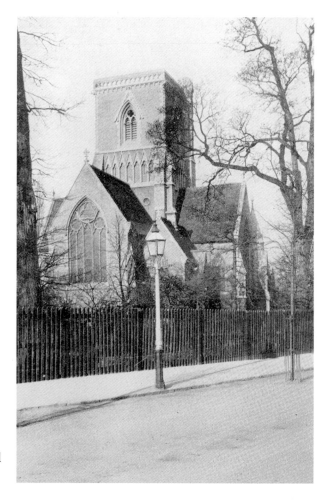

Holy Trinity Church, which stood at the top end of Railway Terrace at the start of Clifton Road.

The Church of St Mark's, Bilton, on a winter morning.

An aerial view of what was Rugby Lower School in Clifton Road – now it is Lawrence Sheriff School.

Little Pennington Street which is just off Corporation Street, looking from Plowman Street towards the town centre.

These three shops once stood in Church Street, very close to The Squirrel pub. They were demolished to make an entrance to what was the open air market, now the Gas Street car park.

A view along Church Street around the turn of the century – not much traffic around, but the horse and carriage are on the wrong side of the road – where's a policeman when you want one?

The trees in Caldecott Park are in leaf in the picture, believed to have been taken just after the turn of the century.

All edges trimmed and grass mown in another view of Caldecott Park.

Another view of Caldecott Park.

One of the avenues in Caldecott Park and some 'new' planting.

Standing on the hill at the end of the village of Newbold, and once surrounded by fields, but now houses, is St Botolph's Parish Church.

The River Avon runs along the bottom of the field below St Botolph's at Newbold.

Eyes down, at the bottom of North Street the Plaza Theatre, and 'Warwickshire's first super cinema', which became the ABC cinema, is now Gala Bingo. Where Hilton's Garage can be seen is now roughly the area of the entrance to the Clock Towers Shopping centre.

A view of Plowman Street, taken in the 50s, showing The Engine pub on the left hand side.

Rugby station. This picture was taken just before the 'Rugby Midland' canopy was demolished on 12 August 1965.

A view of Rugby Gas Works taken from the steps of Number 7 box in 1964.

You might not be able to quite make it out, but there was a sale on at Webbs Outfitters which was at the top of North Street, near its junction with the Market Place.

This is a view taken in April 1958 looking up West Street towards Warwick Street. Little Elborow Street can be seen on the left.

The Tosh – Rugby School's open air swimming pool, built in 1928. It was largely destroyed when the new sports centre was built in 1989.

We are not sure when this picture
was taken exactly, but it a lovely
winter scene of the entrance of
Caldecott Park, off North Street,
Rugby.

An interior shot of Rugby Parish
Church of St Andrews.

A view of the nave towards the sanctuary inside Rugby School Chapel.

A south view shot of Rugby School – check out the fashion!

This railway bridge was an elegant affair and stood in Newbold Road. The first Rugby station would have been to the front left of the bridge. A view of the Avon Mill pub can be seen to the right, through the bridge.

Rugby High School in Longrood Road, taken from the air in 1960.

Market Place in Rugby taken in 1909. Just look at the children's wonderful hats.

You don't see many of these walking down Market Place! This charming picture was taken in around 1900.

Looking toward the Clock Tower, this photograph shows Lawrence Sheriff Almshouses in Church Street, Rugby. It was taken in around 1900.

A view of Brotherhood Hall, now Mood in Gas Street.

The former St Luke's Hospital, which stood in Lower Hillmorton Road, where the Orchard Centre is now situated.

A view of one of Rugby's most familiar landmarks, St Marie's Catholic Church.

The Quadrangle of Rugby School, founded in 1567.

This site in Church Street has long been recognised as a popular spot for Rugby nightclubbers. Today it is known as The White Room after life as the Gas Street Club. Back in the 1970s it was known as Marlowes night club.

A thatched roof is uncovered at Granny's Pies in The Green, Bilton, in 1983.

People and Groups

Miss Bamford was a much loved teacher at Rugby's Westlands School. This picture was taken in 1954.

A rare picture of Thomas Hughes, author of *Tom Brown's Schooldays*, which is set in Rugby School where he taught in the 19th century. A statue of Hughes stands in Barby Road, opposite The Close.

The statue of Thomas Hughes, who
wrote *Tom Brown's Schooldays*, outside
Rugby School buildings in Barby
Road.

This is Roland Bandy whose greengrocers shop, E.R. Bandy, stood in West Street, Rugby. This picture was taken in the 1950s and the shop closed after his death in 1958. The building was demolished to make way for the Corporation Street dual carriageway.

Here are the men of the P Battery 268 Field Regiment, Royal Artillery TA, in 1966. The picture was taken at Tilshead Camp, Wiltshire.

This picture shows P Battery of the TAVR Centre in Rowland Street, Rugby, in about 1954. The military men look smart in their uniforms.

Here are the smiling members of Rugby Women's Air Training Corps in about 1945.

Where there's muck there's brass, so they say, and here is the BTH band with a full set of instruments and a fine uniform. The date is unknown.

Some of the best singers in the town are pictured here in 1931. The group is Rugby Choir, which had obviously been successful in a competition, judging from the trophies pictured in the centre.

An all male domain in the choir of Rugby's Holy Trinity Church in about 1928. The church stood where Trinity Court old people's flats are now situated in Church Street. It was demolished after a fire in 1980.

Dressed in uniforms resembling firemen, all these men worked for Mazda Lamps, BTH, in the early 20th century. Have you noticed that they are all smoking a pipe? Anyone know why?

Looking smart in their uniforms are the musical males of Bilton – all members of the village's brass band in 1913.

With trophies on display are members of Rugby Town Silver Band.

Moustaches were very much de rigeur when this picture of Rugby Town Prize Band was taken in about 1904.

A gathering at Rugby's Roller Skating Rink in Railway Terrace opposite the present Cattle Market site. On the balcony are members of Rugby Town Prize Band. It is thought to have been taken in about 1912.

Musicians from 1921–22 are seen here. They are all members of Crick Band.

Getting ready to play sweet music are members of Rugby Town Band, featured here in the 1940s.

Boy Scouts on parade in the early 1960s coming past what is now Crown House, opposite the council offices in Russelsheim Way.

Where did you get that hat?! These are the girls of the First Rugby BTH Guides in 1920.

This group of likely lads formed Rugby's 25th Abbotts Farm Cub pack back in about 1967.

The men of Rugby St John's Ambulance in about 1960. The St John headquarters were in Regent Place in premises now occupied by a chiropractor's practice.

Don't they look smart. They are members of Rugby Special Constabulary pictured in October 1972.

Taken in the 1940s, this is a picture of the girls from the 7th Rugby Guides.

Choristers from St Leonard's Church, Ryton-on-Dunsmore, are seen here in 1952–53. In the centre of the back row is former Rugby Mayor Cllr Laurie Wright.

The Mayor and Mayoress, Ken and Joyce Marriott, were guests of honour at this meeting of Rugby Winemakers' Circle in 1969. It met at the headquarters – the Rugby Polish Ex-Servicemen's Club in Oliver Street.

Memorable Events

An important day in the life of Rugby's Boys' Brigade when Earl Roberts came to inspect the company in February 1908, possibly at the railway station.

Excitement in Rugby on 3 July 1909 as King Edward VII came to town to open the Temple Speech Room.

The view along Hillmorton Road on the day King Edward VII visited Rugby. In all the excitement it appears that the decorative archway has been put up backwards!

Eyes to the front as King Edward VII inspects Rugby School troops in July 1909. Seen on the far left with a flowing beard is H.A. James, headmaster.

Boys of the Paddox Scout Troop looking spick and span for the visit of the Chief Scout of the district some time between 1950 and 1952. The troop met at Hillmorton Community Centre.

These party-goers from Pennington and Plowman Street in Rugby are celebrating the Queen's Coronation in 1953 at Oakfield Club, Bilton Road, Rugby.

This picture shows a Coronation Day celebration in Rugby on 3 June 1953. It was taken at a fancy dress party at the top of Selborne Road, Overslade.

Pupils from Bloxham Junior School in Rugby celebrate the Queen's coronation in 1953. Each class at the school dressed up to represent a different country. This class represented Australia.

A right royal time was being had by these residents of Deepmore Road, Cherry Grove and Shelbourne Grove. It was a party in 1953 marking the Queen's coronation. The mayor of the day was Cllr Frederick Press, seen in the centre wearing his chain of office.

The weather was obviously chilly for this celebration of the Queen's coronation in June 1953. The revellers were all residents of Mellish Road and Elmore Road.

Children from Mellish Road and Elmore Road, Rugby, in fancy dress to mark the Queen's coronation in 1953.

Ladies and gentlemen of Mellish Road and Elmore Road at the coronation celebrations in June 1953.

A right royal day for these residents of Mellish Road and Elmore Road who donned fancy dress to celebrate the Queen's coronation in 1953.

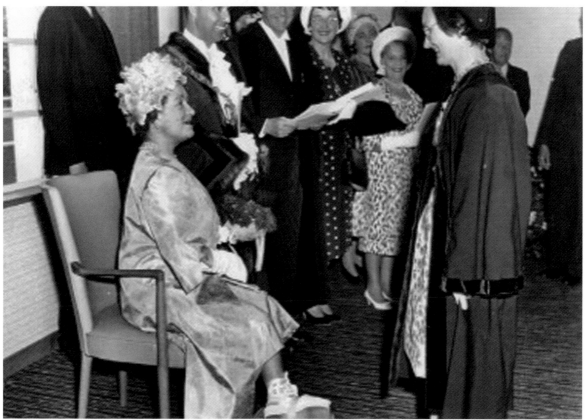

It was a great honour for Rugby in 1961 when the Queen Mother officially opened the Benn Hall in Newbold Road. The special visitor had injured her ankle and a special stool was provided for the royal foot.

These Rugby children are pictured having a right royal time at a commemorative party. It was either to celebrate the 1936 Silver Jubilee of King George V or the coronation of King George VI the following year. The children are from Cambridge Street, Hunter Street and Corbett Street.

This royal flavoured picture is of winners at a fancy dress parade in 1977. It was held in Overslade to mark the Queen's Silver Jubilee.

Smiles all round from these men and women, all relieved that the Second World War was over. It was a VE Day celebration in Rugby in 1945.

This was a historic day for Rugby School when Lord Roberts visited to inspect the CCF in 1906. The large building in the background is the first Rackets Court, designed by William Butterfield and built in 1859.

It's a right royal occasion as Queen Elizabeth and Prince Philip open the new Queen Elizabeth Gates in Barby Road in 1967.

Her Majesty Queen Elizabeth II plants a tree on her visit to Rugby School in 1967.

The Duke of Gloucester visits the people of Rugby in 1988.

More Events

This was the scene every Saturday morning in the 1940s in what is now Bruce Williams Way. The road, which was then a pathway, became a playtime motorway for young drivers of these miniature vehicles.

Fun-loving Long Lawford children take part in a charming May Day celebration in 1957.

This picture shows youngsters celebrating May Day. The children are from Dunchurch Boughton Endowed School, and the picture is thought to have been taken in 1949 or 1950.

Regulars at The Bull and Butcher pub in Ryton-on-Dunsmore will be interested in this shot, which was taken in about 1922.

Fun-loving partygoers pose for the camera before enjoying a dance. The event was held at the Co-op Hall in Chapel Street on 9 October 1952.

These happy people have got their dancing shoes on as they take a trip to the Firs Ball, held in Rugby's Firs Girls' Club. The club was based in what is now Firs Drive, off Russelsheim Way, and the shot is believed to have been taken in the 1950s.

Did you attend Old Bilton Methodist Church Sunday School in the 1950s? If so, you may find yourself in this photo, which was taken on an outing to Skegness in 1959.

Performers at Rugby's famous BTH Rag Week proudly pose for the camera. The picture shows a variety cabaret, which was part of the carnival in aid of Rugby's Hospital of St Cross and is believed to come from either 1938 or 1939.

This picture captures the excitement of the BTH Rag – the forerunner of Rugby Carnival. The girls pictured were office staff at BTH and it is believed to come from 1947 or 1948.

It's not often an elephant pounds the streets of Rugby, but this picture captures the moment when it actually happened. The elephant, which is walking past what is now the Town Fryer restaurant in Church Street, was paraded as part of the BTH Rag Week, and the photograph is believed to come from the 1950s.

Builders of a shop on the corner of Craven Road and Bath Street take a break from construction duties. The men worked for Shillitoe the builders, and the picture was taken in April 1914.

Christmas 1945 and a party for children of employees at Rugby's BTH works. It was just a few months after the war so the food was probably a little sparse.

Back in the 1980s Rugby had its own Live Aid festival in Whitehall Recreation Ground. This couple were among the crowd.

Rugby's Live Aid Festival back in the 1980s at Whitehall Recreation Ground.

Festive smiles abound at this children's Christmas party in the late 1940s. They were all children of members of the St John Ambulance, English Electric Division, in Rugby.

Girls from St Marie's School, Rugby, shaking their tambourines in about 1939–40. The reason for the activity has been lost in the mists of time.

Taking a break from their labours are the girls of Rugby Co-op check office in the late 1940s to early 1950s. The picture was taken at the Co-op sports day held in the Co-op gardens and premises in Bilton Road. It was followed by a dance in the evening.

Staff at Rugby Marks and Spencer enjoy their Christmas party held in the St John Ambulance Hall, Regent Place, in 1954.

Members of staff at Rugby's Marks and Spencer store let their hair down at their Christmas party in the late 1950s.

Rugby's Marks and Spencer staff are pictured at the Bull Inn, Sheep Street, in the late 1950s for a presentation to the window dresser, Topsy Pymm. She is seen with the bouquet. Manager Mr Putt is next to her and his wife is on the other side.

Witches and evil looking cats adorn the walls at the Hallowe'en dance for members of staff at Rugby's Marks and Spencer store in 1957. It is thought the event was held at the Masonic Hall.

Saying it with flowers are a group of girls in the early 20th century at a village May Day celebration near Rugby.

Ruby Murray, pop star of the 1950s, was a big draw at J.T.E. Brown's record shop (now Carvells) in Bank Street, Rugby. Ruby was signing copies of her latest hit, *Softly, Softly*, in 1955 and she was three hours late because she had been recording for Radio Luxembourg. But she made up for it by staying for two hours signing record sleeves.

BTH performed its own musicals with full orchestra. Was this one *The Desert Song*?

The year is unknown, but this was the BTH Rag – a regular fundraiser in town. The females pictured are from the BTH Girls' Club.

This was Carnival Day at Pailton in 1940.

A look into the future at Rugby Carnival in 1978. This float, submitted by Smith Industries Ltd, shows the imaginery 'Return of the First All-British Space Shuttle, 12th July 2001'. It never happened, of course!

A couple of aliens from the 1978 Rugby Carnival float submitted by Smith Industries Ltd. The two unknown ladies were presumably extra passengers on the space shuttle.

Looking like mediaeval princesses, these ladies were all dressed up for Rugby Carnival in 1978.

Rugby Carnival in 1979, and an impressive float of The Wizard of Oz complete with the Tin Man, Lion and Scarecrow, as well as Dorothy and the Wicked Witch of the West and several other characters.

You certainly had to be a card to enter Rugby Carnival for this picture. It was taken in the 1960s or early 70s.

These ladies and gentlemen are in a fancy dress competition in 1953. It was held at St Mark's School in Bawnmore Road, which is now The Crescent School.

The cast of *Stags and Hens*, who performed at Rugby Theatre, hit the town centre in the 1980s.

Hats were definitely the thing when this picture was taken in 1929–30. It shows members of Rugby's St Oswald's Mothers' Union on their annual outing.

Mums from St Oswald's Mothers' Union enjoy a trip to the Wedgwood Potteries in Staffordshire in the 1960s.

Enjoying a Sunday school outing are children from St Andrew's Parish Church, Rugby, in about 1946–47. It was possibly taken in Monks Kirby.

All dressed up are young theatricals from Rugby's Eastlands School in 1940. They are seen in costume for the school play.

All in their finery are Rugby Borough Councillors, partners and friends at the annual civic ball in 1968 – the mayoral year of Ray Holder. It attracted 430 guests, including civic heads from 17 local authorities, plus the Bishop of Coventry and Rugby MP Bill Price. After dinner there was dancing to the Freddie Garth Big Band.

Managers from Co-op stores in Rugby and villages in the area are pictured during a trip to Lowestoft Waveney Food Factory in 1962.

The 1916 Service of Remembrance in Caldecott Park can be seen in this photograph. The houses in Park Road are in the background.

Young men and women enjoy one of the regular Air Force dances in Rugby's Co-op Hall in Chapel Street in either 1948 or 1949.

Christmas was being celebrated here at the annual party for draughtsmen and tracers from Dunne and Co, Sabin, Hart and Partners and G.K. Troupe, all three of which were based in the town. The picture is thought to have been taken in about 1949–50. Dunne and Co were based in Market Place and Troupes were above what is now the Town Fryer in Church Street.

This picture from 1968 shows walkers getting ready for the annual 50-mile sponsored walk between Rugby and Edgehill.

Lucky day trippers from the Rugby Corporation enjoy a seaside jaunt with their families to either Hunstanton or Skegness in 1951.

Sporting

Lads from the late 1950s in Rugby's English Electric six-a-side football tournament.

Taken at the Lawrence Sheriff Arms (formerly the Pig and Truffle and now Midas), in about 1948, when amateur boxers trained there. Pictured are Billy Barber, who became British and England International, Johnny Williams, who became British European Professional Heavyweight Champion, and young Johnny Well Don Scott (Johnny Williams' sparring partner) and Joe Leeming, who became ABA Light Middleweight Champion. Alf Gardner, looking over Joe's shoulder, far right, became Rugby's first amateur boxing judge.

Players from the British Rail Football team at Mill Road lined up for this shot in 1952.

Again, from 1951 or 52, pictured with their trophies are Rokeby Juniors.

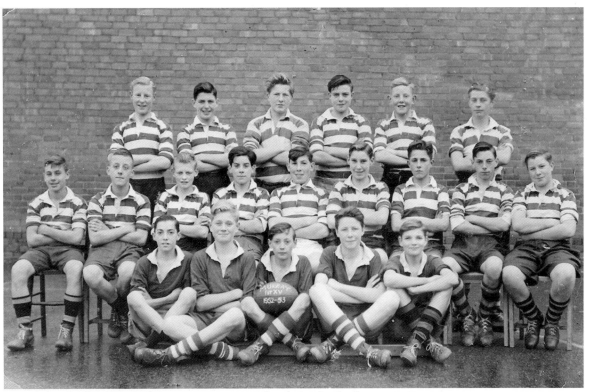

Boys from the first XV rugby team at Murray School, Rugby, in the 1952–53 season.

Members of Rugby Police Boxing Club, which met at the old police station in Railway Terrace.

Look at the super 70s hairdos in this picture of Kingsley Football Club players. It was taken on top of Kilsby tunnel in about 1978.

Descendants of this fine band of footballers may well spot their ancestors. The team were Rugby Central and the picture was taken in 1909. The club still exists today under the title of Rugby Town.

A rugby team from St Andrew's Boys' Club in 1932.

Looking proud with their trophy are members of the BTH Harriers – the forerunners of Rugby Athletic
Club. It was taken in the late 1930s.

Young athletes from Rugby's old Eastlands School make up members of the school's 1st Cricket XI of 1948.

This rugby team are from the 1942–44 season at St Matthew's School in Rugby.

Members of New Bilton Albion FC, pictured during the 1951–52 season outside The Holly Bush in Lawford Road, Rugby.

This is the cricket team of Rugby's old Murray School in 1952, looking very smart.

These smiling footballers are from Rugby's Eastlands School and the picture was taken in 1947.

Young sportsmen from Rugby's St Andrew's Football Club, taken in 1935.

Members of Aston House rugby team from St Matthew's School in the 1948–49 season.

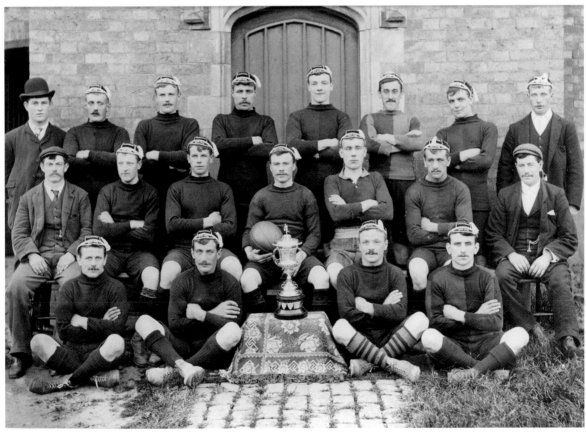

Newbold Football Club in the 1902–03 season when they won the Coventry and District Challenge Cup.

A team from Rugby Lions, possibly in the 1950s.

Thomas Hunter cricket X1 of Rugby in the late 1940s.

Cricketers from Rugby's BTH Girls' Club First XI in 1934.

Sex equality was evident even in 1920 when this picture was taken of the BTH Girls' Club's First X1 cricket team. Presumably, the male pictured was their manager.

Trueloves Football Club of Rugby in about 1951–52.

Young cricketers from Rugby's old Murray School in 1953. Among those pictured is former Rugby Mayor Laurie Wright, fifth from left on the back row.

Time for celebration as members of Rugby's Admirals Junior Football Club receive their awards at the annual presentation night in about 1980.

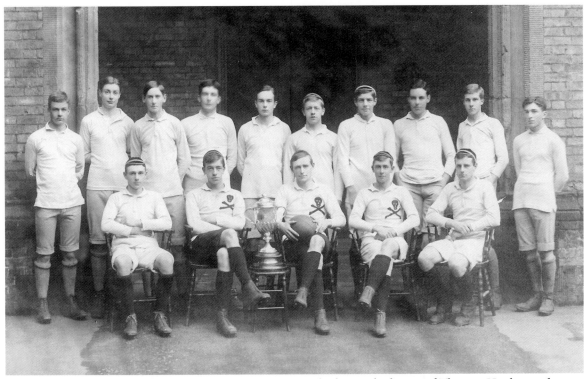

A 1907 team picture of Rugby's School's School House, which was the house of Thomas Hughes and Lewis Carroll. In this year they won the Cock House Trophy, the forerunner of the Rugby World Cup, a competition to find the best team in the school.

These sporting lads from 1957–58 are all members of Rugby's Valley Sports Football Club at the club's first annual dinner at the old Granada Restaurant.

This football team were known as The Griffin Dodgers. The lads belonged to The Griffin pub in Rugby, and the picture was taken in the 1960s.

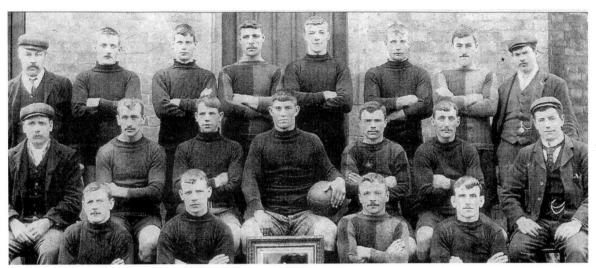

This picture is of Newbold Football Club in the 1901–02 season.

This photograph was taken at the Sheaf and Sickle in Long Lawford and pictures sportsmen from Long Lawford Rugby Football Club in 1890.

Soccer players from the swinging 60s are all lined up and looking smart in this photograph. They were all pupils of Long Lawford Junior School in 1964.

Young rugby players pose for the camera during their 1914–15 season.

Players and Officials from Hillmorton Football Club proudly line up for a team photograph. This shot is believed to come from the late 1940s.

Members of Rugby Town Football Club pose for the camera during their 1949–50 season.

A high level of fitness was shared by these chaps, who were all members of Rugby Falcon speedway team. These keen cyclists are seen at a bike show in aid of the team in 1951. It was at the old Rokeby Club, now the A1 Club in Market Street.

School Photographs

Students from Rugby's old Junior Commercial School in Lower Hillmorton pose for the camera. This picture was taken in 1947.

Keen pupils at Lawrence Sheriff School smile for the camera. The youngsters were all members of class 5c in 1950.

Proud prefects from Rugby's Eastlands School on display. This picture was taken in July 1948.

Staff at Rugby's former Murray School pose for the camera. This shot was taken in the mid-1920s.

These boys from old Murray School in Rugby were caught on camera in 1930–31.

These lads are all members of Rugby's old Murray School XV in the 1930–31 season.

Pupils from Wolston School line up for display. The picture is from the 1920s.

Pupils from Paddox Primary School line up for display. The picture is believed to have been taken in the 1950s.

Children at Clifton-on-Dunsmore School line up for display. The picture is believed to have come from the 1920s.

Girls from the former Dunsmore School look their best for the camera in 1958 – the year before they all left school.

Teaching staff from the former Dunsmore Boys' School in Rugby are seen here in the 1970s.

Youngsters from St Matthew's Infants' School in Little Pennington Street take part in a nativity play. The picture is believed to have been taken in 1949 or 1950.

Pupils at Rugby's old Chapel Street School pose for the camera. The picture was taken in about 1930.

Girls from Rugby's old Northlands Junior School line up for display. This picture is believed to have been taken in 1953.

Young pupils of Tower Lodge private school in Bilton Road in 1958. The building is now Tower Lodge Apartments.

These rounders-playing girls were all pupils of Monks Kirby Primary School in about 1947. They are seen with their teacher Mr Goddard.

Pupils of St Mark's School in Bawnmore Road in 1969. The school is now The Crescent – a private establishment.

Boys of Eastlands School with two teachers, pictured in 1914.

Looking immaculate in their gymslips are girls from Rugby's Eastlands School. The date is uncertain, but it is possibly in the 1930s.

These children were all pupils at Rugby's Eastlands School. It is believed the picture was taken in the 1940s.

Youngsters from Bilton Infant School in 1949.

Pupils of Lincoln House School in 1953, the year of the Queen's coronation. The school stood on the corner of Caldecott Street and Hillmorton Road.

Pupils of Westlands Girls' School in Rugby in 1953–54.

Look at these sweet children from Grandborough C of E School. The picture was taken in 1923–24.

Here are pupils from Bilton C of E School pictured in about 1947. The school building is now Bilton Evangelical Church.

These were students and staff at the Junior Commercial School at Rugby Technical College in 1947. The college stood on the present site of Warwickshire College Rugby Centre in Lower Hillmorton Road. It offered a two year commercial course for girls and a technical course for boys.

Students and staff of Rugby's Junior Technical School, pictured in 1949.

Look at the smiling members of Rugby's old Elborow School in 1930. The rugby playing lads attended the old school in Hill Street.

Pupils from Rugby's St Marie's School smile for the camera in either 1951 or 1952.

Pupils from Dunsmore School for Girls line up on display. This photograph captures a class from 1956–57.

Children from Rugby's St Oswald's School in Lawford Road are captured here in 1974.

Industry and Working in Rugby

This picture, from a postcard, is believed to have been taken in 1908 and shows employees from Rugby's British Thomson Houston leaving work.

An inside view of the BTH works in 1921.

Busy at work are employees of the BTH toolroom in 1924.

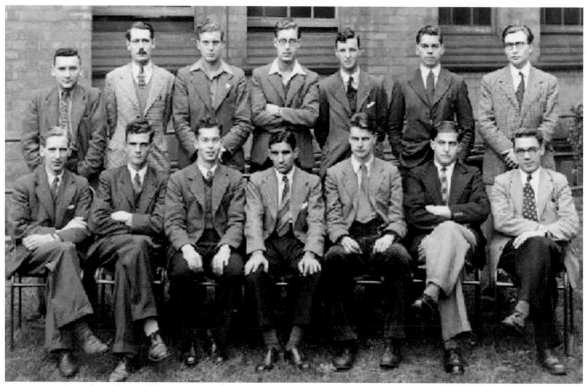

A group of workers from BTH in 1949.

The BTH factory in Rugby where electric torpedoes were made.

Staff from BTH, the forerunner of GEC, pose for the camera. This picture was taken sometime in 1959 or 1960.

It's back to the 60s for this picture, taken at Rugby's BTH before it was taken over by AEI in 1960–61.

Hard at work at Rugby's AEI factory. The date is uncertain.

Employees of Thomas Hunter Ltd. of Rugby, with not less than 25 years' service. The picture was taken in 1929 when the firm celebrated its Diamond Jubilee. The firm built railway wagons and had premises near the Leicester line of the railway station. The only approach to it was from Newbold Road and the path is still known today as Hunters Lane.

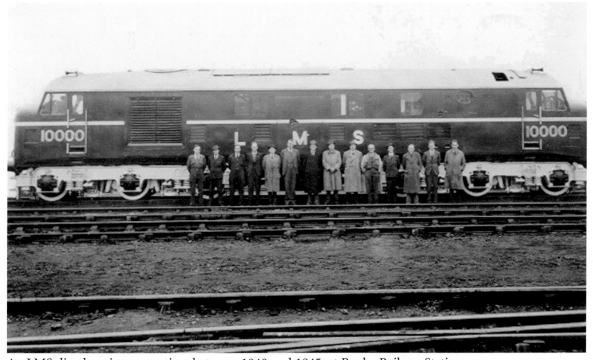

An LMS diesel engine, some time between 1940 and 1945, at Rugby Railway Station.

A diesel engine at Rugby Railway Station in about 1945.

Staff from Rugby's former Granada Cinema in North Street are photographed in 1950.

Do you recognise any of these faces of Rugby District Council? We believe it was taken in the 1960s.

Stichers who worked for rugby ball manufacturer James Gilbert pose for the camera some time between the mid 1940s and early 1950s.

Hard-working employees from Rugby's English Electric Company's Willans Works in Newbold Road line up for the Apprentice of the Year ceremony. This picture is believed to date from the mid-1950s.

Looking hungry before tucking in to their annual dinner are employees of C. Cockerills the builders of Tom Brown Street, Rugby. The event was at the Masonic Hall in February 1957.

The Rugby Advertiser in the Past

Hacks hard at work in the Rugby Advertiser office in Albert Street, Rugby, long before computers were the norm.

Rugby Advertiser editor and managing director of 1926, Mr Sydney T. Watkins (seated) and former manager Mr E.E. Hopewell (left) with ex-editor Mr Frank Betts (right).

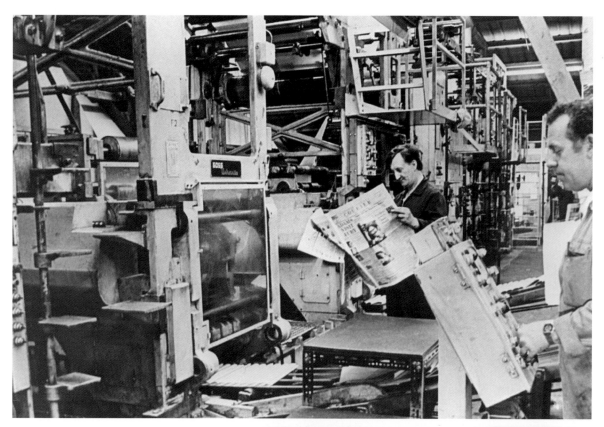

Production staff at the Leamington
Press pour over another edition of the
paper. This photo comes from the
1970s.

Another copy of the Rugby Advertiser
goes to press. This picture was taken in
the 1970s.

Proud staff at the Rugby Advertiser
pose for the camera.

Hard-working staff survey the fruits of
their labours – a copy of the latest
Advertiser.

Hard-working staff at the Leamington
production offices prepare another
edition.

A staff member takes a breather from
producing another copy of the
Advertiser.

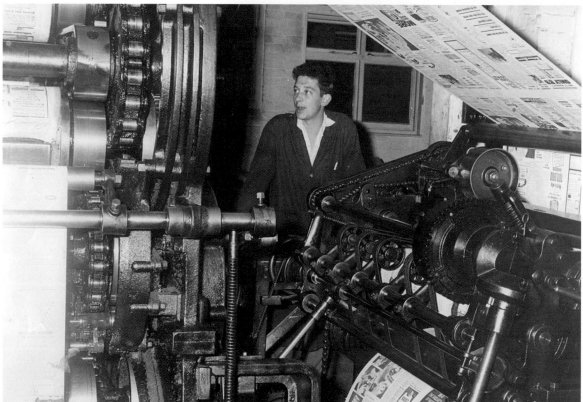

Hot off the press, another copy of the Advertiser.

Pictures of William Ironside Tait, founder of the Rugby Advertiser, and James Hopewell, his son-in-law who succeeded him as owner.

WILLIAM IRONSIDE TAIT,
who founded the *Rugby Advertiser* on March 7th, 1846. He died on New Year's Eve, 1875.

JAMES HOPEWELL,
Son-in-law of the founder, who succee
ownership of the *Rugby Advertiser* o
of W. I. Tait. He was the father of

The Rugby Advertiser offices as they
stood in March 1926.

Workmen deliberate over plans.

Busy staff study the page of another copy of the Rugby Advertiser.

Courier Press, the base for Heart of England newspaper's extensive range of titles, at Tochbrook Road, Leamington.

The Rugby Advertiser Today

Advertiser Editor Peter Aengenheister with Advertisement Manager Ginny Hunter.

Sports Editor Zoe Ashton busy at work, bringing the latest sports news to the people of Rugby.

News Editor Lucie Green makes sure the Rugby Advertiser is first with all the local news.

Reporter Phil Hibble knows how to dig out all the top exclusive stories in Rugby.

Assistant Editor Gordon Birch is also the man behind the Rugby Advertiser's popular Looking Back column.

Editorial Assistant Kate Harris keeps the wheels turning behind the scenes at the Rugby Advertiser.

Happy to help – Senior Receptionist Michelle Allen is a familiar face on the front desk of the Rugby Advertiser reception.

Rugby Advertiser Sales Representative Sian Leyshon makes sure customers' needs are met.

Miscellaneous Photographs

Tragedy for somebody as a house burns. All we know is that it is 'a bit of old Rugby', which was stated on the bottom of the print, but we think it could have been North Street.

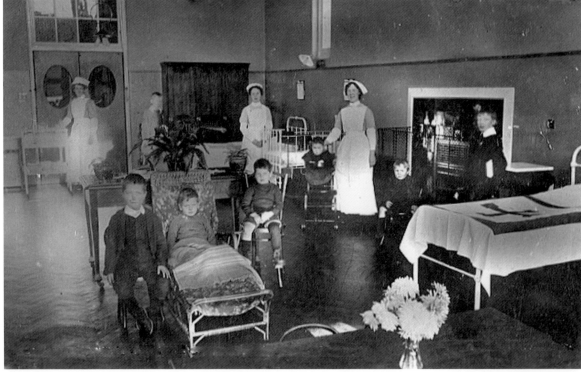

A regular home from home – this was the boys section of the children's ward at Rugby's Hospital of St Cross. Note the open fire complete with guard. It was taken in early 20th century.

He flies through the air with the greatest of ease... Denis Hamnett pictured diving into the water at Newbold Quarry in about 1938. The building shown is the old pump house, which has now sunk.

A scene in 1906 of a shooting match at The Butts by the River Avon, an area of land given over to Rugby School range by Boughton Leigh.

This is the first production at Rugby Theatre photographed in 1949.

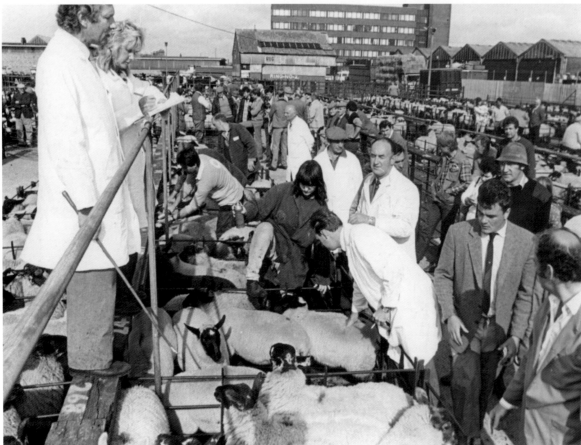

This is a scene from Rugby Cattle Market in 1988. Also pictured is an outside view of Rugby Cattle Market.

This picture, believed to be from the early 1960s, captures a scene from a production of Annie Get Your Gun at Rugby Theatre.

St Andrew's Parish Church can be seen in this photograph taken from the garden of a Rugby cottage in the 1950s.

The War Memorial gates at
Whitehall Recreation Ground.

A group of Rugbeians emerge to see the first gate gently lowered to its new resting place at Whitehall Recreation Ground in 1987.

This is Bilton Green looking very pretty in the late 1950s. Not least among the changes in the landscape are the daffodils, which have been replaced with crocuses.

In the School House garden before going to the Temple Speech Room for Rugby 'speeches' is (from left, back row) Dr Michael Brown, President of the Old Rugbeian Society; Mr A.J. Hunt, Second Master; Sir Edmund Compton, Govenor. Front row: Headmaster Dr W. Hamilton with governors The Rev. M.B. Dewey, Mr J.T. Christie, Lord Parker of Waddington, Sir Alan Wilson and Sir Harold Bibby.

This mini vehicle was part of an operation called 'Holidays at Home' aimed at amusing children who couldn't go on holiday because of the war. The picture was taken at Whitehall Recreation Ground in Rugby in the 1940s.

This is top 70s Rugby band Bus Stop, taken outside the Woolpack Inn (now demolished) in East Union Street. The picture was taken in 1974–75.

Dog owners from the 1960s are featured in this photograph. They are members of Rugby Dog Training Club, and the picture was probably taken on Twickenham Field in Overslade Lane.

Members of third Rugby Boys' Brigade during the mile of pennies collection day for the hospital of St Gross in 1937.

These strikers are from the ASLEF union and were photographed in the 1950s. They are marching to the British Rail loco sheds in Rugby to get their strike pay. The national strike over pay lasted for two weeks.

This is a 2A engine from the loco shed at British Rail, Rugby, decorated with poppies and laurel leaves for a service of remembrance in the loco shed in 1949. It commemorated ex-employees of the Railway.

This gathering marked the retirement of Mr Lewis, a goods agent at British Rail Wood Street goods yard in Rugby in the 1950s.

A busy day at Rugby's bustling market when it stood in Gas Street.

Looking fit and healthy, these ladies are all members of Rugby's St Oswald's keep fit class of 1963. They met in the church hall.

This photograph features Pike's Pure Ices and was taken in the mid 1920s.

Towser the Great Dane takes centre stage in this picture from the early 1950s – he was used to advertise Lassie films at the Regal Cinema in Railway Terrace.

Rugbeians enjoy a talent contest at the former Granada Cinema, now the Gala Bingo Club in North Street, in 1956.

This concert party group was popular around Rugby in about 1936. It was called Bits and Pieces, Hatched, Matched and Patched.

This picture was taken at Rugby's Masonic Hall in the late 1950s and features the Alf Robinson band, a popular act with Rugby's music lovers in the 1940s and 1950s.

Many a Rugby romance started to the accompaniment of this band. They were the Ken Lewis Band and played for dancing in the area in the 1950s.

This is Rugby's Masonic Hall in the late 1950s, and it features Paul Lynden Music. All the members lived in Rugby at the time.

This picture captures the Anthony Lister Band taking a breather while on stage at the old Granada Cinema. The picture is believed to have come from the late 1950s.

This picture captures a performance from the Anthony Lister Band, a popular group, at the Rokeby Club in Market Street. The photo is believed to come from either 1951 or 1952.

Rugby's Freddie Garth Big Band wow the crowds at the former Granada Cinema in North Street in the 1960s.

This picture was taken in 1955 at the Playfair Ballroom, which was on the first floor of Burton's shop in High Street, Rugby.

Jazz was the thing in the late 1950s and Rugby had its fair share. These musicians are seen playing at Club 11, which was upstairs in the Red Lion pub, now Flares, at the end of Sheep Street.

Meet the Julian Brooks Quartet who played for dancing in and around Rugby in the 1960s.